BLAZERS™
Bilingüe/Bilingual

CABALLOS DE FUERZA/
HORSEPOWER

# BUGGIES PARA ARENA/ DUNE BUGGIES

por/by Jennifer L. Marks

Consultora de Lectura/Reading Consultant:
Barbara L. Fox
Especialista en Lectura/Reading Specialist
Universidad del Estado de Carolina del Norte/
North Carolina State University

Capstone press®
Mankato, Minnesota

Blazers is published by Capstone Press,
151 Good Counsel Drive, P.O. Box 669, Mankato, Minnesota 56002.
www.capstonepress.com

*Library of Congress Cataloging-in-Publication Data*
Marks, Jennifer, 1979–
    [Dune buggies. Spanish & English]
    Buggies para arena/por Jennifer L. Marks = Dune buggies/by
Jennifer L. Marks.
    p. cm.—(Blazers—caballos de fuerza = Blazers—horsepower)
    Summary: "Simple text and photographs describe dune buggies,
their design, and uses—in both English and Spanish"—Provided by
publisher.
    Includes index.
    ISBN-13: 978-0-7368-7728-2 (hardcover)
    ISBN-10: 0-7368-7728-2 (hardcover)
    1. Dune buggies—Juvenile literature. I. Title. II. Title: Dune buggies.
TL236.7.M3718 2007
629.222—dc22                                                    2006026109

**Editorial Credits**
Sarah L. Schuette, editor; Thomas Emery and Patrick D. Dentinger,
    book designers; Jason Knudson, set designer; Jo Miller, photo
    researcher; Scott Thoms, photo editor; Strictly Spanish,
    translation services; Saferock USA, LLC, production services

**Photo Credits**
2006 Trackside Photo, 4–5, 6, 7, 8–9, 17, 20, 22–23, 24–25, 28–29
Artemis Images, cover, 16, 18–19
Corbis/Jim Sugar, 26
Getty Images Inc./Kevin Winter, 10–11
Shutterstock/Richard C. Bennett, 21
Unicorn Stock Photos/Jim Argo, 12–13, 14, 15

**The author dedicates this book to her sister, Lisa Marks, of
Cody, Wyoming.**

1 2 3 4 5 6 12 11 10 09 08 07

# TABLE OF CONTENTS

# TABLA DE CONTENIDOS

# CATCHING AIR

The growl of powerful dune buggy engines fills the desert. Zipping up and down hills of sand, one daring driver aims for the biggest dune.

# SALTAR POR LOS AIRES

El rugido de los potentes motores de los buggies para arena se escucha en el desierto. Subiendo y bajando colinas de arena a gran velocidad, un audaz piloto se dirige hacia la duna más grande.

The buggy races up the dune. It launches off the top and zooms through the air. The buggy lands with a bounce and roars off to the next dune.

El buggy sube velozmente la duna. Sale disparado desde la cima y vuela por los aires. El buggy aterriza con un rebote y continúa hacia la siguiente duna.

## BLAZER FACT

The wind shapes sand into dunes. Sand dunes can look like ridges, mounds, and even stars.

## DATO BLAZER

El viento hace que la arena forme dunas. Las dunas de arena pueden tener el aspecto de riscos, montes e incluso estrellas.

Not even the tallest dunes can stop these speedsters. Catching air is what dune buggies do best.

Ni siquiera las dunas más altas detienen a estos bólidos. Saltar por los aires es la especialidad de los buggies para arena.

Catching air/Saltar por los aires

## BLAZER FACT

Drivers try to avoid large dips called "witch eyes" in sand dunes. Buggies can flip if they hit them.

## DATO BLAZER

Los pilotos tratan de evitar grandes hoyos, llamados "ojos de bruja", en las dunas de arena. Los buggies pueden volcarse si los golpean.

## DESIGN

Big tires and lightweight frames make buggies perfect for racing across beaches and deserts.

## DISEÑO

Llantas grandes y estructuras ligeras hacen que los buggies sean perfectos para andar en la playa y en el desierto.

Many dune buggies have smooth, soft front tires. The back tires are tall and wide. Big treads, called paddles, help push buggies through sand.

Muchos buggies para arena tienen llantas delanteras lisas y blandas. Las llantas traseras son altas y anchas. Los dibujos grandes de las llantas, llamados paletas, ayudan a impulsar los buggies en la arena.

Paddles/
Paletas

Dune buggies hit many dips and bumps. Shock absorbers make the ride smoother. Skid plates keep buggies from catching on rough terrain.

Los buggies para arena golpean muchos hoyos y montones de arena. Los amortiguadores hacen más suave el paseo. Las placas de deslizamiento evitan que los buggies se queden atorados en terreno agreste.

Shock absorber/
Amortiguador

Skid plate/Placa de deslizamiento

# REV THE ENGINE

Dune buggies have powerful engines. Many buggies use engines from motorcycles or small cars.

# ACELERAR EL MOTOR

Los buggies para arena tienen poderosos motores. Muchos buggies usan motores de motocicleta o de autos pequeños.

Many dune buggies have air-cooled engines. These buggies drive so fast that the rushing air cools the engines.

Muchos buggies para arena tienen motores enfriados por aire. Estos buggies avanzan tan rápido que el aire que entra rápidamente enfría el motor.

## BLAZER FACT

Dune buggies are so light that the engine doesn't need a lot of gas. They can get 40 miles (64 kilometers) to the gallon.

## DATO BLAZER

Los buggies para arena son tan ligeros que el motor no necesita mucha gasolina. Pueden andar 40 millas (64 kilómetros) por galón.

# Dune Buggy Parts/ Partes de los Buggies para Arena

Shocks/Amortiguadores

Tires/Llantas

Roll cage/Jaula antivuelco

Skid plate/
Placa de
deslizamiento

**23**

# BUGGIES IN ACTION

Buggie races are held all over the United States. Fans love to watch their favorite buggies battle to the finish line.

# BUGGIES EN ACCIÓN

En todo Estados Unidos se llevan a cabo carreras de buggies. A los aficionados les gusta ver a sus buggies favoritos competir hasta llegar a la meta.

Even the U.S. military uses dune buggies to carry spies deep into enemy land. No matter their uses, dune buggies can travel anywhere.

El Ejército de Estados Unidos también usa buggies para arena para transportar espías a territorio enemigo. Sin importar cuáles sean sus usos, los buggies para arena pueden viajar a donde sea.

# ONE BUCKING BUGGY!/
# ¡UN BUGGY BRONCO!

# GLOSSARY

**catching air**—a term for when all wheels of a vehicle leave the ground

**harness**—the set of straps that hold a driver in place

**paddles**—the series of raised ridges across a tire

**roll cage**—the structure of strong metal tubing that protects a dune buggy driver if a buggy rolls

**shock absorber**—a part of a vehicle that lessens the shock of driving on rough surfaces

**terrain**—the surface of the land

# INTERNET SITES

FactHound offers a safe, fun way to find Internet sites related to this book. All of the sites on FactHound have been researched by our staff.

Here's how:

1. Visit *www.facthound.com*

2. Choose your grade level.

3. Type in this book ID **0736877282** for age-appropriate sites. You may also browse subjects by clicking on letters, or by clicking on pictures and words.

4. Click on the **Fetch It** button.

**FactHound will fetch the best sites for you!**

# GLOSARIO

**el amortiguador**—parte de un vehículo que reduce el impacto al conducir sobre superficies agrestes

**el arnés**—el conjunto de correas que sujetan al piloto

**la jaula antivuelco**—la estructura de tubo metálico fuerte que protege al piloto de un buggy para arena si el buggy se vuelca

**las paletas**—los bordes elevados en la llanta

**saltar por los aires**—frase utilizada cuando todas las llantas del vehículo se despegan del suelo

**el terreno**—la superficie de la tierra

# SITIOS DE INTERNET

FactHound proporciona una manera divertida y segura de encontrar sitios de Internet relacionados con este libro. Nuestro personal ha investigado todos los sitios de FactHound. Es posible que los sitios no estén en español.

Se hace así:

1. Visita *www.facthound.com*

2. Elige tu grado escolar.

3. Introduce este código especial **0736877282** para ver sitios apropiados según tu edad, o usa una palabra relacionada con este libro para hacer una búsqueda general.

4. Haz clic en el botón Fetch It.

**¡FactHound buscará los mejores sitios para ti!**

# Index

# Índice